HAPPY HEARTHS AND HOMES

WHERE HEARTS ARE WARMED BY POEMS

By

ROY E. PETERSON

TRICROWN BOOKS

Happy Hearths and Homes
Where Hearts are Warmed by Poems

By Roy E. Peterson

**Cover Credit: Painting, By the Light of the Fireside.
Hugh Cameron, 1867**

*Published on behalf of TriCrown Books by Kindle Direct Publishing,
August 12, 2024*

ISBN: 9798333994240

*Questions: Kindle Publishing or tricrownbooks.com
Available for sale on amazon.com and Kindle.com*

FOREWORD

"Happy Hearths and Homes" is a collection of 101 original poems by the author who has published with this volume 6,100 poems in 88 poetry volumes among 111 books. In my non-compendium books such as this one, my poetry is divided in sections of ten poems. In this one they are: 1.) Love and Romance, 2.) American and Nostalgia, 3.) Humor and Comedy, 4.)Wit and Wisdom, 5.) Inspiration and Fantasy, 6.) Spiritual, 7.) Nature, 8.) Political and Social Observations, 9.) Haiku, 10.) The Good Life/Holidays, and 11.) Sun Tzu and the "Art of War."

I have been a featured writer in several annual volumes of the *Journal of the Society of Classical Poets* and *Western Writers*.

BRIEF AUTHOR BIOGRAPHY

Personally, I am an Award-Winning Singer and retired LTC, US Army, Military Intelligence and Russian Foreign Area Officer. I was the first US Foreign Commercial Officer in the Russian Far East and IBM Regional Manager in the same location. As one of the most educated men in America with 200 post-graduate hours and 3 Master's Degrees. I make no apologies for my logic and views on any subject you wish to name unless it is esoteric science.

Two hundred twenty-nine (229) of my poems have been published by the prestigious Society of Classical Poets of which I am a member. You may read them all by going to their website, clicking on the Member button, clicking on my name in blue and it will take you there.

For a more comprehensive author biography go to the end of the book to the page listed in the Table of Contents.

TABLE OF CONTENTS
Total Poems (101 Originals)

11. Sun Tzu and the Art of War

Notes to the Table of Contents

LS = Love Sonnet.
NS = Nature Sonnet.
RS = Religious Sonnet.
Recovered = Found and Unaccounted Previously
Revised = Primary revision of a previously published poem
SCP = Published by the Society of Classical Poets
SQ = Sonnetesque - Sonnet variations in meter and/or length.

1

LOVE AND ROMANCE

Painting: Couple in the Spring, Carl Hopfer, Munich, 1800's.

ALIENATION OF AFFECTION
By Roy E. Peterson (July 27, 2024)

Texas has no law against
Alienation of affection.
A lover cannot be sued for
The diversion of attention.
Still romancing of a married person
Must be done with caution.
Jealous spouses might murder both
When discovering intention.

HOW MANY?
Love Sonnet #347
By Roy E. Peterson (July 28, 2024)

How many roads must I travel in vain?
How many dreams must I dream to come true?
How many feats of grand legerdemain?
How many ways can I say I love you?

How many times have I yearned for one glance?
How many nights have I wished on a star?
How many days have I searched for romance?
How many songs have I played on guitar?

Each of these deeds are more than a thousand.
The years without you have taken their toll.
Misty eyes dim my sight at the brow's end,
Yet hope beats eternal deep in my soul.

Love is worth all the travails I have known.
Put thou that quote of mine on my gravestone.

LOVE IS YOUR OWN JOURNEY
By Roy E. Peterson (July 2, 2021)

When you fall in love some people
Will not understand.
Love is your own journey
They don't need to know you planned.

Love is for one couple
The whole world can watch and moan.
The roots are intertwined
As the tree of love is grown.

LOVE QUOTES FROM TV SHOWS
By Roy E. Peterson (May 1, 2020)

On the "Good Witch" series,
Starring Catherine Bell,
"You can't have too much love,
Or chocolate," I heard her tell.

Penny in the series, "Lost,"
Characterized her world thus,
"All we need to survive,
Is someone who truly loves us."

On the "Castle" tv series,
The lovers did not use a phrase.
They ended conversations
With the word, "Always!"

Juliet O-Hara on the tv series "Psych,"
Tried to shed a little light.
"Well, I think you deserve more
Than just popcorn tonight."

Mulder on the "X-files"
Was an agent with a task.
He said, "A dream is an answer to a question
We haven't learned how to ask."

"Criminal Minds" ended in quotes
They often wouldn't explain.
"Find the place inside where there's joy,
And the joy will burn out the pain."

Someone tried to give a hint
On "The Gossip Girls."
"Say just three words with eight letters,
And I am yours,"

One said on the "Vampire Diaries,"
Where for life is what they strive:
"You should love the person
That makes you feel alive."

"Love is like an arrow.
It must fly straight and true."
That is not a tv quote.
It's one from me to you.

MY GIRL LIVES IN A WONDERLAND
By Roy E. Peterson (November 18, 2019)

My girl lives in a wonderland
That is known as Dallas.
I must go back to find her.
I call her, Sweet Alice.

Alice in Wonderland
Lives in a crystal palace.
I know I will find her
When I get back to Dallas.

My girl has a husband.
I bear him no malice.
He's the reason for the nickname
I gave her of Alice.

When we get together
We'll share a silver chalice.

ONLY YOU CAN
By Roy E. Peterson (July 30, 2024)

Only you can kiss me the way you do.
Only you can show me a love so true.
Only you can live in the heart of me
Only you can drive me to ecstasy.
Only you can bewitch me with your eyes.
Only you can take me to paradise.

SWEETEST NOTES GO UNSUNG
Love Sonnet #249
By Roy E. Peterson

The sweetest notes of heart-strings go unsung
Waiting for that angelic special one.
Through the world we go with listening ears
Longing for those love chords one never hears.

Where is that one to give us lavish praise?
Where is that one to comfort us always?
We love them and we know they know it.
We are waiting for them to bestow it.

A voiceless sorrow sinks within our heart.
We took the stage, but will they play their part?
A song by Elvis said the stage is bare.
We play on though the emptiness is there.

When empty silence threatens us to drown,
Then that's when they can bring the curtain down.

Poet Note:
1. The song referenced sung by Elvis is "Are You Lonesome Tonight."

THE LIVES OF SOME GIRLS I LOVED
By Roy E. Peterson (July 28, 2024)

When I attended Hardin-
Simmons University,
I met a lot of girls
Who were interesting to me.
Since I had no transportation,
Dating was not so cool.
I had to stay on campus
And just walk around the school.

The first great girl who wanted me
Was named Betty Darnel.
We would walk around the campus
And sit in the chapel.
The second one was studying
To be a nurse named Sue.
Without a car we only lasted
For a month or two.

Jeannie was the co-social chairman
Of my freshman class.
Then the summer break came on
And our love ran out of gas.
When I became a sophomore,
My roommate had a car.
A few times I could use it,
But I could not go too far.

We often double dated,
But we were inhibited.
I could kiss with Bunny,
But our love was so restricted.
Finally, I bought a car
With summer money I earned
By now it was my junior year.
It was time that I learned.

I met Bunny in September,
But the spark wasn't there.
There was a girl one hometown over
Who kisses would share.
On some weekends I would travel
Back the two hundred miles.
She had made me feel loved
And we shared a lot of smiles.

Judy sat beside me
With intent of learning knowledge.
She had transferred to HSU
From a junior college.
Beauty was in her body,
In her face, and eyes and hair.
Secretly I fell in love
While I was sitting in my chair.

I asked around about her,
But each weekend she went home.
I guess I was too timid
To contact her on the phone.

I was surprised when she sponsored
Our Pershing Rifle team.
I got to walk behind her
While I would enjoy the scene.

I decided I would ask her
For a date the next year.
I learned she became engaged,
And then she would disappear.
As a senior I found out
That Judy had been married.
In the summertime
And that doused the torch I carried.

The years have passed by since,
And I still love her just the same.
We have been in recent touch
Despite her now married name.
I learned she could not have children,
So with him adopted two.
I had three blessings of my own
And grandchildren a few.

If she could have had children,
This would be my worst regret.
Now that I have been divorced,
She's the greatest love I met.
I marvel at life's mysteries
And with whom we marry.
So take my tale of wishful love
And find it cautionary.

THE TIP OF THE VOLCANO
By Roy E. Peterson (July 29, 2024)

There are love affairs that should
Be kept a safe secret.
I find I'm in one of those
And I have no regret.
There are secrets in our messages
That no one may know.
That is just the smoke from
The tip of the volcano.

It's hard to keep some secrets,
Though two may have a chance.
Still I find it difficult
To have to hide romance.
My heart has jubilation,
But our love I can't say.
We have to keep it hidden,
But love will find a way.

WOMEN AND ROMANCE
By Roy E. Peterson (July 27, 2024)

Women will swoon at images
Of passionate romance,
One who holds his heart on his sleeve
And dares to take a chance.
Women also are the most likely
Ones to learn to dance.
If men will heed wise words of mine,
Their love life will enhance.

2

AMERICANA AND NOSTALGIA

Painting: Going to Church. George Henry Durrie. 1853

BIB OVERALLS
By Roy E. Peterson (August 7, 2024)

I used to wear bib overalls
When I was still a kid.
I needed them for all the farming
Chores that I once did.

I remember copper buttons
With the trademark, Osh Kosh.
They were assembled in Wisconsin,
As they said, by gosh.

They had little pockets in the bib
To store some things
With bigger pockets side and back
To save my slingshot strings.

When I would go to gather eggs,
The hens would always peck.
Bib overalls protected me
At least below the neck.

BLUE LAWS THEN AND NOW
By Roy E. Peterson (August 7, 2024)

We used to have "Blue Laws"
That were in effect for Sunday.
All the town stores in Texas
Remained closed until Monday.

"Blue Laws" were named for paper color
On which they were printed.
Texas "Blue Laws" still forbid
Sunday sale of alcohol.

Texas kept forty-two items
That can't be sold at all.
There is a lot to be said
For maintaining the "Blue Laws."

EVENNG IN PARIS
By Roy E. Peterson (August 7, 2024)

Since the 1950's, I recall mom's parfum.
How I loved the smell when she wore it in the room.
The bottle was a beauty; glass of cobalt blue.
Evening in Paris label was pretty, too.

That bottle seemed to last her for several years.
She only used a tiny dab behind her ears.
The bottle has become a beautiful antique.
It has a lot of value, since it is unique.

FOOTBALL COMES AGAIN IN FALL
By Roy E. Peterson (July 30, 2024)

Football comes again this fall
Ready for a six-month haul
Of passes received by receivers
Making us the true believers.

Who will be the MVP
Of the quarterbacks we see?
Who will take first place control
And who will win the Super Bowl?

JOHNNY POPPERS
By Roy E. Peterson (August 5, 2024)

I remember Uncle Dale
Had a Johnny Popper.
His John Deere tractor motor
Sure sounded like a chopper.

He bought the new tractor version
In nineteen fifty-three.
It sounded as if it were popping
Popcorn to me.

The motor was 2-cylinder
With twenty-five horsepower.
That was enough to make it
A good cropper and plower.

I could hear the motor popping
Like hard-soft, hard-soft, hard-
Enthusiasts of Johnny Poppers
Hold it in high regard.

MY PARENTS ONE AND ONLY REFRIGERATOR
By Roy E. Peterson (July 31, 2024)

My parents refrigerator
Lasted fifty years.
Bought in nineteen fifty-five
And never stripped its gears.

The freezer compartment contained
Two trays for the ice.
That International Harvester
Surely was nice.

Can you imagine in these days
One could last like that.
It was soda white colored
And easy to look at.

THE ROOSTER ON OUR BARN ROOF
By Roy E. Peterson (July 31, 2024)

The rooster on our barn roof
Shone golden in the sun.
Our rooster was a weather vane,
On the roof he spun.

When I went to feed the chickens,
He would stare at me,
As if to give fair warning:
Let laying hens be.

THE WATER LADLE IN THE PAIL
By Roy E. Peterson (August 6, 2024)

Wanting a drink of water,
I used an enameled ladle
That was in the water pail
Upon the washroom table.

From the cup with the long handle
We would drink cool water.
Then in an emergency
It made a good flyswatter.

WOOD BURNING KIT
By Roy E. Peterson (August 4, 2024)

I remember getting a wood burning kit
Underneath the tree as a Christmas gift.
It had small cork plaques of pictures for me.
I did not know the art was called pyrography.

I loved the smell of wood as I employed the art.
I could only use it when mother took a part.
I still have that kit buried in boxes of old toys.
Woodburning was great for such little boys.

WOOD BURNING STOVES
By Roy E. Peterson (August 6, 2024)

I remember when stoves
Burned wood for their fuel.
Cast iron stoves never
Needed renewal.
I recall stove pipes
Connecting to a chimney.
Some had a ring of decoration,
By Jiminiy!

When I went to grandma's house,
I smelled the smoked room.
Grandpa pulled the lid off,
While the fire would fume.
Then he would put more wood
Into the fire pit.
We kept warm in winter,
No matter where we'd sit.

3

HUMOR AND COMEDY

Film Clip: Short Silent Film, Buster Keaton, 1920.

BEWARE OF THE BEAR
By Roy E. Peterson (August 7, 2024)

If you are walking in the woods
And see some Charmin there,
You had better watch out
For the toilet paper bear.

Only you can prevent forest fires
Says Smokey the Bear.
Why am I the only one
To prevent them walking there?

They show beef jerky commercials
While walking in woods there.
If you are chewing on beef jerky,
They'll attract a bear.

Listen to me my good friend
If walking in the woods there,
Consider what you are doing
And beware of the bear.

BREAKFAST IN BED
By Roy E. Peterson (August 4, 2024)

I never wanted
My breakfast in bed.
I only could imagine
My sheets turning red.
While I was eating toast
With some strawberry jam,
I would not be watching
The spilling of my ham.

When I went to catch it,
The jam would stain my sheet.
I would hop out of bed
With toast upon my feet.
The coffee then would spill
While covers turned brown.
I won't have breakfast in bed.
I say so with a frown.

MEN AND BOYS NEED PICKUP LINES
By Roy E. Peterson (August 4, 2024)

Men must be creative and have
Good pickup lines to score.
The normal and the most used line:
"Where have we met before?"

That may seem a fine flirty line,
But this one makes me sick.
There are so many better lines
From which to choose and pick.

I offer up some other lines
Found on the internet.
At least they are a change in style
For someone you just met.

The second set of every verse
Is my original.
Every girl is different.
You must assess if available.

Without you, my life's like
A broken pencil, it's pointless.
I want to know you better.
I am captured by your dress.

When I got up this morning I sneezed
And God blessed me with you.
You look like you're going somewhere.
Could I go along, too?

Is your dad a baker?
Because you are a cutie pie.
Do you do the things I do?
If not, I'd like to try.

Do you have a sunburn,
Or do you always look this hot?
I may look too good to you,
But I promise I am not.

Are you a Wi-Fi signal? Because
I am feeling a connection.
I think the two of us should go
In the same direction.

You must be named Google.
You're everything that I've searched for.
Walk away with me,
You are everything that I adore.

I think these are some perfect pickup lines
That you should have tapped.
You will either have some success,
Or else you will get slapped.

MY NIGHTMARES ARE NOT LIKE OTHERS
By Roy E. Peterson (August 4, 2024)

My nightmares aren't like others.
There are no monsters to see.
They're my first day attendance
At a university.

I rummage through my desk,
But I cannot find my schedule.
I don't know where to go to class
For my first day of school.

This dream often comes to me
In August and September.
How many years it's happened
I really can't remember.

I know it may seem funny
That I'm feeling so hopeless.
But it feels like a nightmare
For I wake up feeling stress.

One other nightmare I have
Is of a market gauntlet.
Emerging on the other side
I can't find my wallet.

THE BEE AND ME
By Roy E. Peterson (August 6, 2024)

As I was standing on my porch,
I felt the hot sun try to scorch.
Upon my ceiling was a bee
Looking for shade just like me.

I told the bee he could not stay
On a table I found my spray.
I aimed the spray up in the air.
Half of the spray fell on my hair.

I saw the bee fall to my feet.
The spray was warm, I felt the heat.
I ran inside to take a shower.
I could have died from the spray power.

THE LAST TIME I RODE A BULL
By Roy E. Peterson (August 4, 2024)

Mickey Gilley was a singer
And country musician.
His Honky Tonk in Pasadena,
was his addition.

Now this was Pasadena, Texas,
That the cowboys love;
Not the one in California
We are speaking of.

The last time I rode a bull
Was at Mickey Gilley's place.
I climbed up on the bull that bucked
At a most fearsome pace.

The cowboys and the cowgirls
All cheered and clapped their hand.
The bull then sent me sailing
Straight forward towards the band.

The last time I rode a bull
Was in Mickey Gilley's place.
I still have the scar to prove it —
I landed on my face.

THE EXTERMINATOR
By Roy E. Peterson (July 27, 2024)

My wife and I were arguing again at home,
Soon I overheard her call on the telephone.
She had placed a call for the exterminator.
"Do you kill rats and bugs, whichever is greater?"

Just bring to me the poison. Take it off your shelf.
I will do the extermination for myself.
I began to worry and I began to fret.
Was the call meant for me and was it a real threat?

For days I didn't eat at home or drink anything.
Every day I wondered what tomorrow would bring.
It is safe to say I am among the living.
Did she kill the pests with poison she was giving?

WEST TEXAS EARTHQUAKE
By Roy E. Peterson (July 26, 2024)

Who has ever heard of
Earthquakes in West Texas,
One that shakes the stomach
And the solar plexus?
Today as I was having
My constitutional on the pot,
As I was defecating,
My toilet began to shake a lot.

Puzzled, I began to wonder
As the walls began to shake,
Was it something I had done
That had caused an earthquake?

If my walls fell down,
I could just imagine personal scenes
Today I'll take it easy
And not eat anymore pinto beans.

WEST TEXAS EARTHQUAKES REDUX
By Roy E. Peterson (August 4, 2024)

West Texas had one hundred
Earthquakes in three weeks.
This time that it happened
The oil wells sprung leaks.

One hundred fifty years ago
They cane alive,
When Goodnight and Loving
Had made a cattle drive.

WRITING MY OWN OBITUARY
By Roy E. Peterson (July 27, 2024)

I think I should write my own obituary;
Not leaving to relatives or the mortuary.
Who knows about their spite, or they decide to write,
After I am gone and will remain out of site.

William Ziegler had one that's written by his kid.
It talked about his life and funny things he did.
Besides children and grandchildren in his registry,
William "left behind the potted meat industry."

Mary (Pat) Stocks' son wrote her obituary
Read at her funeral in the sanctuary.
At the age of 94 she had had enough.
Mary "left behind a hell of a lot of stuff."

Johanna Scarpatti loved "The Wizard of Oz."
She told daughter, Sue, what to write in the first clause.
When they picked up the paper, this is what they read--
Sue obeyed her wishes, "Ding, dong, the witch is dead."

Harry Stamps appeared to be a confirmed foodie.
He hated lots of things and sometimes was moody.
His daughter wrote words after discussing his dregs,
"He had a life-long love affair with devilled eggs."

Scott Entsminger rooted for Cleveland Browns always.
To paraphrase the write up of his final days--
He requests six Cleveland pallbearers stand in line
So they can let him down for one final time.

I read these obituaries and I'm afraid
Of what my kids may write and what they might have said.
I have some words that might be wise and tender.
"He lived his own way and has returned to Sender."

4

WIT AND WISDOM

Painted Greek Cup: Pythia, Oracle of Delphi. 440 BC.

ALTERNATIVE SENIOR LIVING
By Roy E. Peterson (August 7, 2024)

With the cost of nursing homes
Continuing to rise.
I have some great advice to give
All our senior guys.
The daily cost of nursing homes
Is now two hundred bucks.
One can quickly go broke in one
And therein lies the crux.

There are many options
That a senior should consider.
Stay forever on a cruise ship,
Or motel resider.
Cruise ships have great food
And I know that they are cheaper.
Motels cover all the needs
At sixty bucks, a keeper.

Either choice is better,
There will be no need to debark,
If you are on a cruise ship,
So stay there when it parks.
Pick a nice motel that serves
Breakfast, lunch and dinner.
You even get a free maid service.
I call that a winner.

ARTIFICIAL POETRY
By Roy E. Peterson (August 4, 2024)

I will never use AI
To write my poetry.
I would rather make mistakes
And know it came from me.

I take pride in knowing that
At least it's me who tried,
Not some AI program bot
Upon which I relied.

Poet Note:
I would be surprised if there are still some out there who do not know that AI stands for artificial intelligence generated by computer programs.

BLOOD SUPPLY SHORTAGE
By Roy E. Peterson (July 28, 2024)

They tell me there's a shortage in our blood supply.
If we do not donate soon somebody may die.
The problem is we never know who that may be.
Although that leaves it vague, it could be you or me.

Our donations of blood could have a real big boost,
If hospitals and doctors would disclose its use.
I may have a solution when our blood is retrieved,
Write to both the parties who gave and who received.

CATBIRD SEAT
By Roy E. Peterson (August 9, 2024)

They said I'm in the catbird seat.
I don't meow and I don't tweet.
I feel as if I'm on a swing.
I can't fall off or it will sting.

I take my potshots like in skeet
For I swing in the catbird seat.
They say I have the upper hand,
But that depends on where I land.

FAVORED SECOND TOES
By Roy E. Peterson (August 2, 2024)

When the second toe on your feet
Is longer than the big toe,
You are like Leonardo,
Venus, and Michelangelo.
Italians thought it creative;
They took it from the Greek.
If you had such a longer toe,
They thought it strong, not weak.

They both considered such a one
Would make them a great leader.
When such a woman walked in sandals,
Everyone would heed 'er.
Fifteen percent of the population
Have a Greek toe.
The ancient Greeks once called such things
The "Golden Ratio."

Poet Note:
The Golden Ratio denoted by the Greek letter phi (Φ), is a Greek discovered mathematical ratio related to geometry and commonly found in nature, art, and architecture. This irrational number equals approximately 1.618, and has properties that fascinated scholars, sculptors, artists, and architects for centuries. It replaced the ancient Egyptian Rule of Proportion.

FIERCE LOVE
Love Sonnet #348
By Roy E. Peterson (August 2, 2024)

If you write about me, here's where to start,
I have a fierce love bound within my heart.
I have loyalty for God and country.
My love's forever to one loving me.

God's love for me I know is eternal
He has saved me from the fires infernal.
My country right or wrong, I will protect,
But our government I may not respect.

My lover must show me great fealty
Whether virtual or reality.
They must want to give as much as the get.
The love for me must be without regret.

Those with loving hearts are real romantics.
Poets 'loving words are found in semantics.

MCDONALD'S NEEDS AN ADULT PLAYGROUND
By Roy E. Peterson (August 8, 2024)

I think that McDonald's needs
An adult playground,
Where they could watch each other
As they play around.
Women in bikinis could jump
On the trampolines.
Men in bathing suits could lounge
And they could see the scenes.

They could slide into
The plastic balls like children do.
The pits would be much bigger
To accommodate the crew.
They could have a strong swing
And slide into some water,
Especially in summer
When it is getting hotter.

The kids would keep their own playpens
To keep them out of trouble.
They would then be supervised
By staff that they would double.
Adults would work off calories
And eat more Big Macs there.
I should call their marketers
And my idea share.

NEVER BE TOO BUSY
By Roy E. Peterson (August 9, 2024)

Never be too busy
For the things that matter.
Trust depends on you.
It's something you can shatter.

When a fine friend has helped you
Get to where you are.
Be quick with your helpfulness
In support of their star.

PLAYING ON THE INTERNET
By Roy E. Peterson (August 6, 2024)

Who would play Casino games
On the internet
Where one can win no money
If they make a bet?
The ad placed on the screen
Says anyone who joins,
After the first ten plays,
Will win a trillion coins.

The offer shows that winning
Is easy as pie.
Coins spinning from the wins
Are meant to catch your eye.
I cannot imagine
Playing for such action.
If there is no money,
Where's the satisfaction?

THREE KEYS OF WRITING CLASSIC POETRY
By Roy E. Peterson (July 26, 2024)

I want to share three keys
Of writing classic poetry.
With message, rhyme, and meter,
It is satisfactory.
All three are important keys
To which one pays attention.
You can be a classic poet
With these keys retention.

There's some disagreement
As to which is most important.
Unless one uses all three keys,
Poems are discordant.
My order of importance
Is what I provided you,
Though teachers of the classic art
Reverse the order, too.

I put the message first,
Because why else would I write one.
I ensure my message
Is covered before I am done.
I check for its consistency
And power of my prose.
Have I included all the facts
Before I write my close.

When I read a classic poem,
I look first for the rhyme.
If it's inconsistent or lacking,
It's a waste of time.
Rhymes in classic poems
Are like a veritable flavor.
Transfixed in my mind
They are like a taste I can savor.

Meter is the third key
Making poems mellifluous.
The fine flow of words is like
A beat that pounds within us.
If one doesn't feel like dancing
And the beat seems to elude,
Then count the syllables
While you are writing your etude.

5

INSPIRATION AND FANTASY

Painting: Calliope. Eustache Le Sueur. 1852-55.

DEMENTIA IN ABSTENTIA
By Roy E. Peterson (July 28, 2024)

He was diagnosed as suffering dementia.
He often saw ghosts, his loved ones in abstentia.
When he watched a movie on his television,
Even reruns seemed new that he could envision.

Since he had lived alone for thirty years or more,
His dreamworld seem perfect and better than before.
The nurses in his new home made sure he was fed.
They would turn out his lights when it was time for bed.

He would talk with new friends, especially the dames.
Every day the same ones, but he would ask their names.
On somedays he might have a visitor or two.
They seemed like the ghosts of the relatives he knew.

EVENING IS FOR REFLECTION
By Roy E. Peterson (July 27, 2024)

Evening is for reflection;
It is the end of the day.
Did I help somebody out
Or sent them on their way?

Was my day filled with kindness
Or was it filled with mean.
Did I defer to others
Or did I make a scene?

I pray that tomorrow
I will become wise and smart.
Help me to others
And show my love in my heart.

FEAR IS LIKE A LITTLE CHILD
By Roy E. Peterson (August 9, 2024)

Fear is like a little child that
Cannot be left alone.
It continues tugging at our hearts
Until it is grown.

Like that little child, fear needs
Our constant attention.
If we don't think of it,
Fear can't keep retention.

It is the little things in life
That seem to worry us.
Fear plays on our emotions
And causes us to fuss.

"Fear not," said the Lord,
"For I am with you always."
You are not forgotten,
If you trust in that word phrase.

FIREBRAND
By Roy E. Peterson (July 24, 2024)

I have been called a firebrand
And a fire starter.
It goes with what I learned in life
That made me much smarter.
I may be an arsonist
But won't set your house on fire.
I start social wildfires
When a person conspires.

I include the political
In the social domain.
I love to burn bad "houses" down
To see what would remain.
No one can douse my flame out,
Because I will teach the truth.
I have been a fire starter,
Since the days of my youth.

HAVE YOU EVER WALKED ON CLOUDS
By Roy E. Peterson (March 23, 2024) Recovered

Have you ever walked on clouds?
Have you ever dared to dream?
Have you ever seen your reflection
In a cooling mountain stream?

Have you ever taken first steps
So you may climb a mountain high?
Have you done your best in life,
Or at least gave it a try?

Have you struggled on the pathway
To attain what you believe?
The motto of my school class was
"To aspire is to achieve."

When you're walking on the clouds,
You have reached the mountain crest.
You have not only dared to dream,
But you kept going through the mist.

MY GIRLFRIEND FROM THE PAST
By Roy E. Peterson (August 3, 2024)

My girl of eighty-one said that
She fell over dead.
She has the scar to prove it
Incised on her forehead.
Although we live about
Four hundred miles apart,
She is my love from college
Who is always in my heart.

Somehow, they revived her
And the doctor's took a look.
It must have been an aneurism
According to the book.
For years we have been talking
And this problem left me shook.
At least we still communicate
By using our Facebook.

I still call her my girlfriend,
Although she has a husband.
It is a cataclysm to which
I have become accustomed.
I often dream of her at night
And think of her each day.
Someday we'll be together;
That is something that I pray.

OLD FOLKS ENTERTAINMENT IN THE PAST
By Roy E. Peterson (July 26, 2024)

What did old folks do
Before television and radio?
What about without computers
And watching the video?

In the 1800's, solace for old age
Was the rocking chair
Or reading books like poetry
And some telling stories there.

We have made a lot of progress
For old folks since days of yore.
Perhaps the olden days were golden
With oldsters reading more.

SOCIETY OF CLASSICAL POETS GREATS
By Roy E. Peterson (August 4, 2024)

The Society of Classical
Poets are the greats.
They write rhyme and rhythm
Messages to which I relates.

Evan Mantyk, President,
Critiques when we make mistakes.
He carefully will choose which poems
To publish or forsake.

C.B. Anderson once had his
Own good gardening show.
His poetry reflects his knowledge
And what we should know.

Andrew Benson Brown may be
Greatest of us all.
His words are highly educated,
Some I can recall.

The Mistress of Alliteration
Is **Susan Jarvis Bryant**.
Often when I read her poems,
She's culturally defiant.

Margaret Coats of Harvard
Earned her Ph.D. degree.
She interprets French and Chinese
And can write great poetry.

Sally Cook was nominated
For a past Pushcart Prize.
I have not seen her poems lately,
How nature will surprise.

Cynthia Erlandson writes with
A precious loving touch.
When I need to change my mood,
Her poems will help me so much.

James Sale sends us superb poems
While writing in the UK.
His portrayal of Dante's epic
Has so much to say.

Dr, Joseph Salemi
Is our gift from Italy
When his parents immigrated
In nineteen thirty-three.

James Tweedie is a pastor who
Writes his poems with precision.
His words are often subtle
Referring to religion.

Perhaps one of the keenest minds
Is of Brian Yapko
He began writing when
A lawyer in New Mexico.

Of course, I place myself on
The top ten poet list.
I think others like my poems,
But then I'm an optimist.

These are among the greatest poets
I have ever read.
Sometimes I read a poem by them
Before I go to bed.

Poet Note:
1. **Evan Mantyk**, President, listed first. The next ten are listed alphabetically. Including Evan and myself the list above is twelve.
2. I also like **Warren Bonham, Joshua C. Frank, Daniel Kemper, Norma Pain, and Gigi Ryan** for a total of 17.

SUCCESS REDEFINED
By Roy E. Peterson (August 9, 2024)

Success is not a grade
That's applied to a test.
Success is helping others
Achieving their quest.

Success is measured by
Each one doing their best.
Success is feeling good
When it is your time to rest.

THE SS-ALBACORE (218)
By Roy E. Peterson (August 8, 2024)

One of the most successful submarines
Of the Second World War
Was commissioned in 1942,
The SS-Albacore.
One of the eighty-nine crew members
Was a Texan, Leonard Moss.
Who came from Lubbock, Texas,
And listed as an MIA loss.

For two years the Japanese Navy
Should have feared the Albacore.
Then it sadly had disappeared in action
In nineteen-forty-four.
The Albacore sank ten ships
With the aircraft carrier, Taiho.
Seventy-nine years later
The remains were found near Hokkaido.

The wreck of the Albacore
Was found by Japanese researchers.
In twenty-twenty-three the Albacore
Sub story emerges.
The sub was identified by new portholes
And new radar mast.
The relatives of the SS crew
Have final closure at last.

[
Poet Note: Lu Moss Shirley contacted me about the find,

6

SPIRITUAL

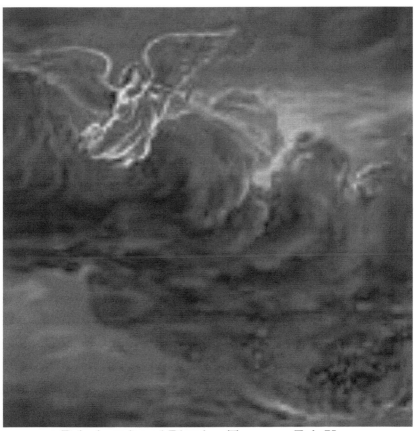

Painting: Angel Blowing Trumpet. Fair Use.

A PROMISE MADE SHOULD NOT BE BROKEN
By Roy E. Peterson (July 31, 2024)

A promise made should not be broken.
A trust is kept in one who cared.
A secret is a word not spoken.
A love is a thing to be shared.

A hope is there for the heartbroken.
A belief is for those prepared.
A faith is there for the outspoken
A prayer is when we are ensnared.

EARTH IS BUT A STEPPING STONE
By Roy E. Peterson (August 9, 2024)

Earth is but a stepping stone
Along a path we tread.
Our final destination's
Somewhere up ahead.

We only see darkly
Like through a smokey glass.
Then we'll find a firmer place
When our life will pass.

Get ready for tomorrow.
Someday it will come.
With the angel chorus
Our instruments we'll strum.

I SLEEP BENEATH MY PRAYERS
By Roy E. Peterson (August 9, 2024)

When we go to sleep as children,
We have a certain dread.
What else could be hiding
Beneath our quilted bed?
We have our parents double check
Nothing is hiding there.
They pretend to look for us,
Because they really care.

There are so many of us
Who have unfounded fear.
We love to hear those words from
friends,
"No on else is here."
I used to fear the monsters
Hiding beneath the stairs
Now I trust in Jesus
While I sleep beneath my prayers.

LIKE THE HOMING PIGEON
By Roy E. Peterson (August 2, 2024)

The homing pigeon is a fascinating bird.
To their sense of direction we have all concurred.
Pigeons can be taken hundreds of miles away.
They will fly straight home and never go astray.

I only can imagine how they make their choice.
Are they so dependent upon the master's voice?
The sun does not explain it. They can fly at night.
They must a GPS that can guide their flight.

Christians have GPS like the homing pigeon.
Heaven is our home, because of our religion.
When my life is over, I will not stay alone,
Then like the homing pigeon, I will fly back home.

SAIL ON IMPERION
By Roy E. Peterson (August 7, 2024)

Sail on, Imperion,
Into the darkest of nights.
Sail on, despite lashed by
The trolling troublesome sea.
Sail on, in search of that
Great indomitable light
That this ship of souls
Shall be safe in eternity.

Like Ezekiel
In fiery chariot borne
Through vague vapors of time
While transcending fierce foam,
So, listen for Gabriel
Who'll be blowing his horn,
To welcome the weary
To his heavenly home.

THANK YOU, SUN, MOON, AND STARS
By Roy E. Peterson (July 31, 2024)

Thank you, sun, for our dark night.
Thank you, moon, for weaker light.
Thank you, stars, for shining bright.
Thank you, Lord, that we're alright.

Sun, you shine your light on me
During the day so I can see.
Your light makes the plants to grow
From the seed we farmers sew.

Moon, you make me feel romantic
Shadows shifting look gigantic.
We see your face is looking down
Smiling when your beams hit the ground.

Stars, above you seem to squish
My hope when I make a wish.
Still, when love is in the air,
My love and I will stare up there.

Lord, I thank you for your love
And all the marvels up above.
Lead me with they guiding light
That removes the darkest night.

THE AGE OF THE DRONE
By Roy E. Peterson (July 31, 2024)

FIFTH TRUMPET: LOCUSTS FROM THE BOTTOMLSS PIT
Bible: Revelation 9: 9-10 (New King James Version)
(The locusts) "…had breastplates like breastplates of iron, and the sound of their wings *was* like the sound of chariots with many horses running into battle. They had tails like scorpions, and there were stings in their tails."

Officially we entered
The Age of the Drone.
It has been two decades
Since testing drones were flown.
We entered the drone age,
Several years ago.
Now they're used for warfare
And targets as we know.

Deadly unmanned vehicles
Have brought death and pain.
They've been aimed at Israel
And at the Ukraine.
They have killed some leaders
Of ISIS and Hamas,
Some have been used against
The Russians in response.

Apostle John who wrote
The book, *Revelation,*
Prophesied that locusts
Would wound every nation.

He said that their breastplates
Would be made of iron.
Wings whirred like chariots;
Tails of a scorpion.

I believe John prophesied
The end of the world
With the seven trumpets
As mysteries unfurled.
He could only conjure up
From weapons he knew.
Drones make perfect sense
After the fifth trumpet blew.

Reading Revelation,
Trumpets number seven,
Till the final trump
Tor the kingdom of heaven.
One need not believe prophecies
Christians have known.
But the world's more dangerous
The Age of the Drone.

THE DEVIL'S REALLY DOWN HERE
By Roy E. Peterson (August 4, 2024)

The devil's really down here
To steal some hearts and souls.
He tries to get ahead
By loosening controls.

The devil does his dances
While singing his devil song.
He always is a winner,
When we play along.

He whispers to the Christian,
"You have nothing to fear.
Just plan to get along,"
He whispers in our ear.

Inaction is the handmaid
Of the devil's plan.
He wants to neutralize us
Any way he can.

THERE IS POWER
By Roy E. Peterson (August 9, 2024)

There is power from the inner
Strength we hide inside.
There is power in the faith in God
With whom we shall abide.

There is power in our purpose,
As our sins we cast side
There is power in our prayer to God,
Who will be our guide.

THIS TOO SHALL PASS
By Roy E. Peterson (August 8, 2024)

When you suffer sadness
And your mind's a morass,
The Lord is there to tell you
That this too shall pass.
The storms still up their fury,
Their darkness hides the sun,
But the Lord reassures us,
Be patient till it's done.

Be calm, O heart, through
Despair and deepest grief.
Time tells us tomorrow
Will someday bring relief.
As nature cures itself
Like the watering of grass,
Here is your consolation,
That this too shall pass.

7

NATURE

Painting: Fishing, Robert Duncanson, Mid-1800's.

AUTUMN'S ALARMING WINDS
By Roy E. Peterson (August 9, 2024)

While autumn's alarming winds blew,
The leaves of trees were talking too.
The maple in embarrassment
Was turning red as leaves were spent.

The oak began to wear a frown,
As all its leaves were turning brown.
The apple tree had tales to tell,
"I think that gold suits me quite well.

The wind then shifted to the cold
And blew away the leaves of gold.
Bereft, befuddled, and de-leaved,
The trees for leaves departed, grieved.

AUTUMN IS FOR WALKING
By Roy E. Peterson (August 9, 2024)

Autumn acorns falling from a tree.
While we'd walk in autumn endlessly.
The squirrels scurried quickly up the tree,
Then stared at us disapprovingly.

We laughed and we chattered, just we two.
While the scared squirrels were chattering, too.
The squirrels were scolding us without doubt.
Autumn is great for walking about.

FLOWERS FOR EVERY MOOD
By Roy E. Peterson (July 30, 2024)

Flowers in my garden are there for every mood.
Colorful creations were seen from where I stood:
Red roses for the fire that's burning in my heart;
Blue violets for the sadness when we're apart;

Marigolds for golden times I spend with you;
Dancing daisies determine if my love is true;
Bluebells beating time while waving in the wind.
Pansies closing petals as nights the light rescind.

Bluebells beating time while waving in the wind;
Pansies closing petals as nights the light rescind.
My garden flowers keep changing every hour,
Providing perfume increasing mental power.

HEATHER IN THE MOOR
By Roy E. Peterson (August 9, 2024)

The purpled heathered ridges
Used to hide me in the moor.
When hunting for the rabbits,
I could glide across the floor.
Time has a way of changing
Perspectives we have seen.
Like dark clouds in the heavens
With silver rain between.

How many rabbits did I shoot?
I guess that I've lost count.
Now that I have grown older,
A rifle I can't mount.
I used to hunt the rabbits
While traipsing o'er the moor.
But now I guess that heaven
Has evened up the score.

HONEY NEVER SPOILS
By Roy E. Peterson (July 29, 2024)

Honey has home healing properties
That are natural
Like healing throats, wounds, and burns,
It's antibacterial.
Honey has antioxidants
That supports healthy brains.
Honey helps allergies
With local pollen from the grains.

Honey never spoils,
It can stay good three thousand years.
Edible in Egyptian tombs,
Was tasted without fears.
Honey is a preservative
That lasts for centuries.
Honey's long-lasting power
Is shown in documentaries.

One teaspoon of homey before
Going to bed at night
Will provide the brain with tryptophan
That makes one sleep tight.
Now read about bees and see
What their story illumines.
Bees are the only insects
Producing food for humans.

I HAVE WAITED FOR SEPTEMBER
By Roy E. Peterson (August 9, 2024)

I have waited for September
When the stars shine silver white;
When the sun with trepidation
Chases off the cold of night.
That's when farmers seek to harvest
All the golden grain that grows;
When man and beast shall shiver
From their midriff to their toes.

I have waited for September
And the stacking of the sheaves;
The shelling of the ears of corn
With the turning of the leaves.
Time to dig up potatoes
Growing in my humble garden.
Time to pick up the pumpkins
And the veggies ere they harden.

There is something in September
That gives me a strange desire.
Time to pick the crimson apples
Trom the trees that seem like fire.
The harvest moon hangs high and huge
Above fulsome farmer's fields.
The farm family says a thankful prayer
For a good yearly yield.

There is something in September
As the world starts shutting down;
While the chilly wind creates on trees
A brightly colored crown;
When the farmer hauls to market
All the good grain he has grown;
And remembers from the springtime
All the seed that he had sewn.

I have waited for September
With my final harvest done.
All the kindness I've shown others
And the victory's I've won.
I await my final tally;
Additions and subtractions
That satisfy my sated soul
From all my interactions.

NATURE LOVES TO SHARE
By Roy E. Peterson (August 9, 2024)

Nature loves to share
___though one finds other malice there
Nature loves to give
___thus showing us how we should live.
Glory of a flower
___is sensed in it's perfuming power
They no longer glower
___when the rains give them a shower.

Nature loves to share
___the produce that is grown out there.
The more that Nature gives
___the more that Nature lives.
We owe so much to nature
___with variegated nomenclature.
Thank you, Nature host,
___for giving us the most.

TEXAS WINDS AND TREES
By Roy E. Peterson (August 3, 2024)

The Texas winds are blowing
As my treetops scrape the ground.
I wonder why they are not breaking
When I hear such sound.
Their roots must have grown so deep
And water helps them to bend.
The branches must be flexible
As my trees cope and fend.

If you have been to West Texas,
The winds get mighty high.
They whistle through the treetops
As the wind is blowing nigh.
I should ask the winds to stop
And say so with a sigh.
Perhaps when it is nighttime
The winds will finally die.

THE HERMIT SQUIRE
By Roy E. Peterson (July 30, 2024)

Far away upon a mountain
Lived an ancient hermit squire.
Where forests gave him wood to count on
For his cabin fire.

City folk sometimes would see him
At the local grocery store.
They might see him at a trash bin
Foraging for more.

People living in the canyon
Talked to him, if he'd permit.
Nature though was his companion
As revered by that hermit.

WE LOVE OUR HONEY BEES
By Roy E. Peterson (July 29, 2024)

We all know busy bees will pollinate our plants
With their sticky leggings, our life they will enhance.
Bees pollinate about one-third of the food we eat,
Like fruits, nuts, and vegetables with their pollen feat.

Bees produce tiny bits of honey in their life.
Just one-twelfth of a teaspoon for all of their strife.
When they work together, though, they produce a lot.
Winnie the Pooh will thank them for their honey pot.

Bees do communicate through their dancing powers.
The perform a "waggle dance" to find best flowers.
Just like remembering different flower places,
Some bees can recognize all our human faces.

Did you know bees are colorblind to the color, red?
Bees see ultraviolet, but red is black instead.
Did you know that bees have a built-in GPS?
They use the sun and magnetic field for success.

8

POLITICAL AND SOCIAL OBSERVATIONS

Photo: Purple Heart Medal with Miniature Ribbon

A BLACK LADY
By Roy E. Peterson (July 24, 2024)

A black lady of some renown
Who once had slept with Willie Brown,
She made her way.
She was a good lay.
The donkeys gave her their crown.

BEWARE THE CONSEQUENCES OF ELECTION
By Roy E. Peterson (August 10, 2024)

A woman who decided
To run for president
Thought illegal aliens
Should vote like residents.

She had no knowledge of
The world's geography,
Who also was defective
In knowing world history.

She picked a running mate
Who was derelict in his duty,
When he was a member
Of the US Army.

There must be some misspelling
When his name is used.
I have seen Waltz and Walz.
I am so confused.

I think the proper spelling
Of his last name must be Walz.
That is because I believe
He doesn't have the balls.

How could either one of them
Have risen so far?
Their goal is to take over,
So she can be a czar.

HALLMARK MOVIE MYSTERIES
By Roy E. Peterson (August 3, 2024)

Although I really do like
Hallmark movie mysteries,
Only women are the lead
Detectives in the series.
They are shown as serious
Everyday persona
With a pretty face and body
Cast as a Madonna.

Candace Cameron Bure,
Laurie Laughlin, and Chabert,
With Alison Swensen
And Kellie Martin are seen there.
Then I add Jill Wagner
And Emma Thompson to the list.
I could add several more
But I think you got my gist.

The settings for the stories
Are in small town locations.
Antique buyers, Bakers,
Librarians by vocations.
They are average women
With a smart and active mind.
Men play the second fiddle
In each series you will find.

Poet Note: Also Brook Burns, Brook D'Orsay, and Danica McKellar.

IF I WERE SECRETARY OF THE US ARMY
By Roy E. Peterson (August 10, 2024)

If I were the Secretary
  of the U.S. Army,
I would cancel programs
  of such stupid blarney.
I'd appoint a new
  U.S. Army Chief of Staff.
Then we would get rid of
  the jokers and the chaff.

We would work together
  and make our next bold stroke.
We would cancel all programs
  spewing words of woke.
Then we'd begin to phase out
  anyone who's queer.
The army must not tolerate
  them we'd make clear.

We would restore the great names
  of the Army Posts.
Like Confederate General's names
  as the hosts.
Efficiency and valor
  would be our watchword.
The real chains of command
  no longer would be blurred.

IRRELEVANCE OF RACE
By Roy E. Peterson (August 6, 2024)

It is personal to inquire
About one's ancestry.
I can find my DNA
On any race registry.

Still the Bureau of Statistics
Wants to assess my race.
I wonder if the time has come
To put race in its place.

First, the Bureau does not keep track
Of blacks mixed with the whites,
Or any other racial mixture
Any one recites.

Instead they put them in the category
They mark as black.
That keeps the numbers skewed
And they are clearly out of whack.

Forget now offensive words
Like mulatto and quadroon,
And with half-breed and mestizo,
As well as octaroon.

We have so many interracial
Children being born.
I think the racial concept now
Is one that is outworn.

I think I have created
A much better racial plan.
I think it's time we called
Everyone all American.

LAWFARE
Reference: The AMAC Magazine cover, August 2024.
By Roy E. Peterson (August 10, 2024)

I saw the great term, "lawfare,"
On the cover of a magazine.
It signifies the warfare on Trump
On the pages written in between.
The article discloses the features
Of the sinister plot to get Trump.
The democrats employ lawfare
For legal charges on him to dump.

The lawfare by the democrats
At all levels weaponized the law
To persecute "our President"
And throw him in jail as their last straw.
They intend to undermine
Trump's reelection, as they confess.
While imperiling the American
Constitution in the process.

Poet Note:
AMAC Magazine, August 2024. Included in the article on page 27, the author, Shane Harris, states: "Biden accidentally gives away the game."

NO FONDUE IN FOND DU LAC
By Roy E. Peterson (August 10, 2024)

Something must be lacking
In Fond du lac, Wisconsin.
Maybe it's the Swiss cheese
That has become rotten.

There is no fondue
That can be found in Fond du lac.
It is the lacking of the fond
That suffered an attack.

OLYMPIANS
By Roy E. Peterson (July 28, 2024)

We are the world's best athletes
With a claim to fame.
We congregate together
Neath the Olympic flame.
We vie to be champions
Awarded with the gold.
We represent our countries
Whose stories will be told.

We are the hard workers
Through blood, and sweat, and tears,
We compete and dare not cheat,
After such a long four years.
We are the Olympians
With heart, and strength, and power.
The few will be the winners
In their finest hour.

REAP THE POLITICAL WHIRLWIND
By Roy E. Peterson (July 29, 2024)

In our nation's politics
Among sinned and less sinned,
Whoever votes for democrats
Shall reap the whirlwind.
The rest of we Americans
Shall suffer from the stain.
We have to make America
Become great again.

THE LAND THAT USED TO BE
By Roy E. Peterson (July 18, 2024)

There was a land that used to be
With fertile fields and boundless sea,
Where people felt that they were free
To live in brave fraternity.

A land made of milk and honey
Where they could earn earnest money.
Somewhere it was always sunny
And the world was often funny.

This land required evidence
With ID for their residents,
Where once they chose wise Presidents
And laws were made with precedents.

This land protected innocents.
Investigating incidents.
A land of great magnificence
That vetted all the immigrants.

9

HAIKU

Photo: Antique Japanese Painting, Kakejiku
Public Domain.

BEYOND THE SHADOWS
By Roy E. Peterson (August 3, 2024)

Beyond the shadows.
When the moon no longer shines.
Only owls observe.

HOW DO I LOVE THEE
By Roy E. Peterson (August 4, 2024)

"How do I love thee?"
I cannot count all the ways.
Like flower petals.

JULIET CRIES OUT
By Roy E. Peterson (August 4, 2024)

Juliet cries out,
"Wherefore art thou Romeo?"
"On the ground. I fell."

LONELY SUMMER BREEZE
By Roy E. Peterson (August 5, 2024)

Lonely summer breeze
Springtime love has gone away.
One less star tonight.

MY MERCIFUL MUSE
By Roy E. Peterson (August 3, 2024)

My merciful Muse
Grant me your great golden gifts.
Spring gives me flowers.

NATURE SUSTAINS US
By Roy E. Peterson (August 6, 2024)

Nature sustains us.
Hydrogen and oxygen.
It's in the waters.

READING WINTER NIGHTS
By Roy E. Peterson (August 3, 2024)

Reading winter nights.
Vision brighter than the light.
Kerosene lamp lit.

SNOWFALL SURPRISE
By Roy E. Peterson (August 3, 2024)

Whistling winter wind.
Trees have no leaves for boughing.
Snowfall mid autumn.

TAURUS MET CANCER
By Roy E. Peterson (August 2, 2024)

Taurus met Cancer
Then arrived a Gemini.
Photographing stars.

WHERE THE SIDEWALK ENDS
By Roy E. Peterson (August 3, 2024)

"Where the sidewalk ends,"
Perhaps there you'll find more friends.
Read Silverstein's books.

10

THE GOOD LIFE INCLUDING HOLIDAYS

Painting: By the Light of the Fireside. Hugh Cameron. 1867

COLUMBUS DAY IS WELL DESERVED
By Roy E. Peterson (August 9, 2024)

On October the 12th, in 1492,
Columbus found new land with his intrepid crew.
Natives did not understand men could be so white.
Or how such ships with sails could navigate the
    night.

As decades go by, Natives are getting restless.
They want to do away with it, so they profess.
It was a great accomplishment against all odds.
Columbus, Discoverer, deserves all our lauds.

Columbus Day is a day that we remember.
Each year it's the second Monday in October.
So let us celebrate and let us not deter.
Let's us keep Columber Day on our calendar.

HALLOWEEN FIREWORKS
By Roy E. Peterson (August 4, 2024)

Fireworks for Halloween,
What could possibly go wrong?
Trick or tret could have new meaning
If we went along.

Why don't we have some fireworks
To shoot on Halloween?
Can you imagine cauldrons
With witches in between?

Put fireworks beneath their pot
Before they stir their stew.
Like dynamite it could explode
And cover them with brew.

The black cats would be quivering
And hiding neath the porch.
The ghosts that some folks see,
The fireworks would scorch.

The dogs would all be howling,
But they'd do it anyway.
I think we should have fireworks
For much more fun that day.

HALLOWEEN IN AUGUST
By Roy E. Peterson (August 4, 2024)

We are barely into August,
But I saw a store sign.
Happy Halloween it said.
Did I lose track of time?

It was stuck on the masthead
Of the former Dollar store.
I looked in through the window
Where I saw costumes galore.

Two full months to go,
I wonder open every day?
Who would buy their candy now
For that happy holiday?

HAPPY HEARTHS AND HOMES
By Roy E. Peterson (July 24, 2024)

How happy are the hearths and homes,
Where hearts are warmed by poems;
Where they can read great poetry
As through pages they can comb.
My mother read them all to me
When I was but a child.
As we sat near the fireplace,
My mind was running wild.

It was often in the evening
Before I went to bed,
Fairies found in nursery rhymes
Were dancing in my head.
Dear Dr. Seuss had just begun
To write when I was young
There was lazy daisy Maizie
Who had a lying tongue.

How merry are the memories
Of eves that long passed by
While I looked at the pictures
With an ever-widened eye.
I loved to see illustrations
Of little people scenes
The I would amble off to bed
And see them in my dreams.

LABOR DAY WORKERS
By Roy E. Peterson (August 10, 2024)

I never understood
Why people work on Labor Day.
Isn't it for laborers
And national holiday?

The second thing that I don't get
And fail to understand,
Why is it such a great sale day a
All across our land?

The big stores make a lot of money
On each Labor Day.
The sales are quite fantastic
While the workers make good pay.

I know there are workers kept
In the convenience store.
The gas stations and fast joints
Are visited galore.

They could close convenience stores, i
If all the workers grump.
The people still would get their gas
From the auto-pump.

Now that I'm retired
There is no labor facing me.
I suppose I'll just enjoy
Another day for free.

PURPLE HEART DAY (AUGUST 7)
By Roy E. Peterson (August 10, 2024)

I found that Purple Heart Day
In on August seven.
It is for their valor
And blood the men have given.

All have suffered wounds
And some have suffered loss.
They all deserve the ribbon with
"For Military Merit" embossed.

THANKSGIVING TURKEYS
By Roy E. Peterson (August 4, 2024)

Thanksgiving is when all the turkeys go to hide,
Except for my relatives I invite inside.
On Thanksgiving day again we all get to meet.
Some of them are jokers and some just like to eat.

I listen to their stories that never get old,
Like going pheasant hunting in the snow and cold.
Then we retire to watch NFL football games
Followed by the parlor fights with calling of names.

RECOGNITION DAYS ON OUR SEPTEMBER CALENDAR
By Roy E. Peterson (August 10, 2024)

Did you know our calendar has a Patriot Day?
That is the basis for our American Way.
It is in September upon the 11th day.
That is a good day to put your flag on display.

On September 20, there's a recognition day,
For the POW and for the MIA.
Then on the 29th, that is Gold Star Mother's Day.
September offers many opportunities to pray.

THE PLACE FOR PETS ON HALLOWEEN
By Roy E. Peterson (August 10, 2024)

When it is Halloween its best
To keep the pets inside.
Cats and dogs need safe places
In which they can hide.
The cats will shriek, the dogs will howl
With knocking at the door.
But don't show them the ghosts and goblins
With the things they wore.

They might decide to charge
The smiling Jack-o-lanterns.
It would be their fright to see
The candle-lighted patterns.
A dog might decide to attack
A monster or a witch.
And he might take exception
To the trick or treaters pitch.

VISITING A HAUNTED HOUSE
By Roy E. Peterson (August 10, 2024)

When I was a teenager,
There was a haunter house.
My friend and I snuck in,
We were quiet as a mouse.

We knew the house had ghosts
And the inside long unseen.
The night that went visiting
Was on Halloween.

We crept us the staircase
That was dilapidated.
Every time it made a squeak
Was something we both hated.

We finally made it up
To the top the stairs.
If there were any ghosts,
We'd catch them unaware.

We looked into a bedroom,
As a ghostly shape appeared.
Since it was just there floating,
It was what we had feared.

We ran down the staircase
And then fell from our pell-mell.
We ran home to our mothers
Like a bat out of hell.

11

SUN TZU AND THE ART OF WAR

Photo: Sn Tzu Statue. Deed-Attribution 4.0 International.

SUN TSU'S "THE ART OF WAR"
By Roy E. Peterson (July 25, 2024)

Best Interests of the State

The Art of War is of vital
Importance to the State.
It is the road to ruin
Or the road to being great.
He will win who knows just
When and when not to fight.
Move with stealth and keep plans
As impenetrable as night.

Whosoever wishes to fight enemy
Must first count the cost.
Build your opponent a golden bridge
To retreat across.
Prolonged warfare never
Benefited any nation.
You must carefully assess
Every situation.

We can't enter alliances
Until were acquainted
With the designs of our neighbors,
One's which could be tainted.
A kingdom that's been once destroyed
Can never be rebuilt.
The dead cannot be brought back
To life once blood has been spilt.

The greatest victories are those
Which require no battle.
The greatest secrets are kept
By those who will not tattle.
Generals who don't covet fame
And do not fear disgrace.
Are jewels of the kingdom
And are worthy of embrace.

Preparation for Battle

Foreknowledge cannot be gotten
From ghosts and spirits.
Obtain it from the people
Who are the closest to it.
Plan what's difficult while easy,
Do what's great while small.
Defense is the time for planning
The attack upon them all.

Trust your men as much as you
Trust your own beloved son,
Then into deepest valleys
They'll follow until war's done.
Treat soldiers with righteousness,
Justice, and benevolence.
The army will be united
When showing them confidence.

If you would know the enemy
You first must know your mind.

If you know them both,
You'll win a hundred battles you'll find
Find a way to put a wedge between
Their sovereign and leaders.
Pretend weakness. Make him arrogant
Before proceeders.

If your opponent has a temper,
Seek to irritate him.
If he is feeling at his ease,
It is time to bait him.
Supreme excellence is breaking
The enemy's resistance
Without a war with their battles
Caused by his insistence.

In the Battle

Sun Tzu's main principles of war
Begin with the surprise.
Attack the enemy from
Your positions of disguise.
Moving forces quickly
Is one key to their survival.
Surprise is masking forces
Before their arrival.

Be extremely subtle,
Even seem to be amorphous.
Be soundless as can be
And appear mysterious.

The whole warfare secret comes
In confusing the enemy,
So that he cannot fathom
What will lead to victory.

When the enemy is relaxed,
Then make them toil harder.
When the enemy is eating well,
Destroy their larder.
In the midst of chaos,
There's also opportunity.
Believing in yourself first
Is the key to victory.

Begin by seizing something which
Your opponent holds dear;
That will make him amenable
To your will and his fear.

One mark of a great soldier is
He fights on his own terms.
He disdains attacking
And any compromise he spurns.
If the mind is willing,
The flesh could go on and on
Without a great many comforts
Until the threat is gone.

As the opportunities are seized,
They will multiply.
Great result can be achieved
By small forces that defy.

In war, avoid that which is strong
And strike at what is weak.
Appear weak when you are strong,
And seem strong when you are weak.

All of warfare is best based on
The power of deception.
Appear to be faraway
When ready for inception.
The enemy will provide
The means for his own defeat.
Our own defenses must be
The best that they cannot beat.

Make him take the bait you offer
And don't fall in his trap.
Use your spies and intelligence
To make of him a sap.
If you fight with all your might,
There is a great chance of life;
Conversely, death is certain
If you hide when there is strife.

Convince him there's little to gain;
His enthusiasm will wane.
One cannot savor the benefits
Who does not know war's pain.
Some roads must not be followed,
Some armies not be attacked.
Some towns must not be besieged,
Some positions not be whacked.

Leadership

Ponder and deliberate
Before your first move or stay.
Rewards for good service
Should not be deferred a single day.
Praise the soldiers and the future
When things are looking bright.
Tell the soldiers nothing
When the outlook's dark as night.

If soldiers are punished before
They've grown attached to you,
They'll never be submissive
And be useless as a crew.
If the words of the leadership
Are not clear and distinct,
It is the fault of officers
And they will become extinct.

The worst army calamities
Arise from hesitations.
Skilled leaders maneuver enemy
To bad situations.
Energy is likened to
The bending of a crossbow;
Decision to the releasing
Of a trigger and the arrow.

When your army's crossed the border…
Burn your bridges and boats,

Each soldier then is clear
Retreat is not an antidote.
Do not use your troops unless
There is something to be gained.
Move not unless you see
An advantage can be obtained.

Conclusion

These are the words of Sun Tzu
That were written about war.
His nine principles are solid
For few have said much more.

Sun Tzu's Essentials for Victory and Dangerous Faults:

1. "Thus we may know that there are five essentials for victory: (1) He will win who knows when to fight and when not to fight; (2) he will win who knows how to handle both superior and inferior forces; (3) he will win whose army is animated by the same spirit throughout all its ranks; (4) he will win who, prepared himself, waits to take the enemy unprepared; (5) he will win who has military capacity and is not interfered with by the sovereign."

2. "There are five dangerous faults which may affect a general: (1) Recklessness, which leads to destruction; (2) cowardice, which leads to capture; (3) a hasty temper, which can be provoked by insults; (4) a delicacy of honor which is sensitive to shame; (5) over-solicitude for his men, which exposes him to worry and trouble."

U.S. Army Nine Principles of War Since 1921:
In the order I remember them (SUMOOMESS)

1. Surprise
2. Unity of Command
3. Mass
4. Objective
5. Offensive
6. Maneuver
7. Economy of Force
8. Security
9. Simplicity

To That List I Add:

1. Observation
2. Intelligence
3. Communication
4. Superior Firepower
5. Superior Technology
6. Mobility

BIOGRAPHY OF ROY E. PETERSON
LTC, U.S. Army, Military Intelligence Retired

Photo: Captain Roy E. Peterson. Can Tho Vietnam, 1972.

LTC Roy Peterson served as an Assistant Army Attaché in Moscow during the peak of the Cold War Years from 1983-1985, as the first U.S. Foreign Commercial Officer in the Russian Far East for the U.S. Department of Commerce with dual duty as a Visa Issuing Officer for the U.S. Department of State, and as the first IBM Regional Manager, Vladivostok, Russian Far East (1993-1995).

He was Commander, Portal Monitoring, On-Site Inspection Agency in Votkinsk, Russia and Commander of the 5th Military Intelligence Company, 18th Military Intelligence Battalion, 66th Military Intelligence Group.

LTC Peterson was trained in Russian, German, and Vietnamese and used all three languages in their respective theaters of operation.

LTC Peterson is a recognized international trade and Russian political/military consultant. Roy was a recent faculty member with the University of Phoenix teaching global business, marketing, sales, management, military intelligence, unconventional warfare, and international trade.

Roy Peterson is a poet, songwriter, and award-winning bass voice singer.

Writing Credentials

LTC Peterson has had published more than 90 books, over 20 extensive secret intelligence studies, over 100 intelligence reports (unavailable), 2 MA theses, and 2 Institute publications. Throughout life he has written monographs, business proposals, and engaged in marketing, for which he has international credentials. He has written over 100 country, rock and gospel songs.

Military Intelligence Credentials

Analyst, National Security Agency
Phoenix Advisor MR IV Corps, The Delta, Vietnam.
Analyst, Defense Intelligence Agency.
Commander, Military Intelligence Company, Germany.
Manager, Army Security Clearances.
1st Army Staff Intelligence Advisor, Pentagon.
Selected to replace Ollie North on Security Council.
Presidential Rep. to Russia, On-Site Inspection Agency.
Army Attaché, Moscow.
Executive Officer, Intelligence Collection Unit
Honor Graduate, US Army Russian Institute.
Russian language fluency.
Human Intelligence Coordinator, 1st Gulf War.
Awarded Legion of Merit, Bronze Star.

Academic Credentials

BA, Hardin-Simmons, MA University of Arizona.
MA University of Southern California.
MBA University of Phoenix.
Ph.D., passed written and oral exams and remains ABD.
Defense Language Institute, Russian.
Graduate, U.S. Army Command and General Staff College.
Faculty Member, University of Phoenix.
Faculty Member, University of Maryland.
Faculty Member, University of Arizona.
Faculty Member, Western New Mexico University.
Faculty Member, Travel University International.
Graduate Assistant, American Government, Texas Tech.

Business Credentials

President, HPO International and TriCrown International.
VP, International Trade Company,.
VP, Investment Company.
VP and COO, Construction Development Company,.
VP Management Company.
Sold trucks to Russia.
1st USDOC Foreign Commercial Officer in Russian Far East.
1st IBM Manager in Russian Far East.
Taught International Trade and Global Business Management.
Director New Business Development for ENSCO.
Wrote operational and technical proposal for EG&G on
        Strategic Arms Limitation Talks Contract.
President Export Company.

BOOKS AND PUBLICATIONS
AUTHORED BY ROY E. PETERSON
(Poetry-88/Other Genre-23/Total-111)

Poetry Books (Also See Political Poetry)

A Child's Home Companion: Poems Children Love
A Poet's New Perspective
All American New Holiday Classic Poems: 100 + Poems for Christmas…
Alien Inspired Verse: Poetry from the Universe
Alpen Splendor, Mountain Grandeur
Always Means Forever: Poetry So Clever Until the Twelfth of Never
America Needs Adult Advice
American Country Poetry: From the Prairie to the Parlor
American Classic Poetry: Poetry for the Majority
American Gold Classic Poetry: If it doesn't Rhyme
American Heartland: Poetry, Wit, and Wisdom
American Heritage Poetry Collection
American Patriot Salute
Angels All Around Us: A Great Garden of Verse
A Pink Moon in April: Poetry from the Periphery
As the World Burns: Poetry by the Fireside
Autumn Echoes: Poetic Treasure Trove…
Blazing Stars Like Flaming Darts: Classic Poems for Classy Hearts
Beauty Begets Emotion: Rhymes of Love and Devotion
Before I Go to Bed: Poetry for Dreaming
Between Darkness and Light
Beyond the Back Seat: Coming of Age Nostalgic Treat
Christian Poetry for the Heart and Soul: My Best Classic Christian Poems
Cassic Poetry Begets Reverie
Classic Poetry Renaissance: Rhyme and Meter Make it Sweeter
Common Sense with Uncommon Sensitivity
Cultural Conservation Companion: Clever Poems for Smart Homes
Democratic Party Down the Rabbit Hole: Descent into Political Madness
Destiny Awaits Me/While I Write Poetry
Dreamers Dream While Poets Scheme: Poets Pursue the Theme
Eternal Spring: Poetry and Promise
Every Heart Gets Lonely
Fables from the Funny Farm: Follies, Frolic, and Fun/Vol 1
Fables from the Funny Farm: Poetry of Wit and Charm/Vol 2
Feet on the Ground: Heart in the Sky
For Love May Find You: Poetry with Passion

Grains of Sand: Poetry by the Sea
Guardian Angel: All My Tomorrows
Guide to Self-Publishing Poetry
Happy Haunting Halloween: Olde and New Classics
Happy Hearths and Homes
Harmony and Discord in an Atonal World: Revelations…..
Hearts and Clouds
Heaven in a Wild Flower/Poetry's Innate Power
In the Garden of My Heart
Love is Made in Heaven/Romance is Made on Earth
Love That Lasts Eternally: Poetry of Romance and Mystery
McCamey Memories We All Share: Nostalgic Poems…
Merry Christmas and Happy New Year Poems
Memories Made Inside Cannot Be Denied
My Best Classic Poetry Collection: Arrows Sent in Your Direction
My Heart Has Not Forgotten: Where'er Thine Feet Have Trodden
My Lady of Light Awaiting Her Knight
Mystery Has an Accomplice: Poems You Won't Want to Miss
Mystery of Poetry
Out of the Shadows: My 110 Best Nature Poems
Peace in My Valley
Poems for Happy Times Treasury: My Own Selected Best Classical Poetry
Poems for the Ages: Sailors, Kings and Sages
Poems from the Heart/Melancholy Times Year for Poetry That Rhymes
Poetry Knocking on the Door: Classic Rhymes
Poetry is Like a Salve; When It is All We Have
Poetry is Passion: Truth and Time in Classic Rhyme
Poetry is the Music of the Heart
Poetry When Nights are Stormy: Classic Poems to Warm the Heart
Race Relations Objective Perspective Poetry
Riveting Romantic Love Treasury: Vol 2 My Own Selected Best Classical Poetry
Shadows on the Garden Wall
Show Me the Moon
Songs from a Sultry Soul
Sonnets for Moonlight Serenades
Sonnets from the Inner Sanctum: Poetry for Posterity
Sonnets from the Mellow Breeze: Great New American Love and Romance Sonnets
South Dakota Classic Poems: From Prairie Country Homes
Southern Comfort from Me: New Classic
Spirit Inspired Verse
Texas Stardust
Texas Trail Dust: Cowboy Campfire Collection
The Art of Persuasion

Top 100 Classic Poems of All Time
Treasury of Wit, Wisdom and Advice: Vol 3 My Own Selected Best Class Poetry
What Captures the Mind
What the Heart Proposes: The Poet Discloses
When I Think of Heaven: Inspirational Sonnets, Soliloquies, Songs…
Where Love Dares to Go: Pathways Only Poets Know
Where the Foxes Play: Poetry to Read When the Fur Flies
While the Wind is Whistling Through the Sylvan Glen
Winter Casts Her Spell: Autumn Says Farewell
Whither My Love: Treasury of Great Classical Love Poetry

Poems Published by Western Poetry

Writers of the Purple Sage (May 2013)
Tucson Sunday Morning (February 2014) (Song)

Poem Published by Hardin-Simmons University

Night Storm. Quiet Thoughts. Hardin-Simmons University, 1963.

Winning Poem in Oprelle Contest, June 2021

I Never Felt Like I was Poor, August 2021, Rise Up, *Oprelle*.

History

American Attaché in the Moscow Maelstrom
Fight of the Phoenix
Soviet Intelligence Process (Out of Print Monograph)
The Velvethammer: Lieutenant Colonels Get Things Done

Historical Fiction

From Chapultepec to Castle Gap
Hitler's Secret Jet Designer: Jet Invention, Austrian Connection…
Iron Ikon: U.S. Foreign Commercial Officer Duty in the Russian Far East
     (Out of Print)
Russian Bears/American Affairs
Russian Romance: Danger and Daring (Out of Print)

Humor, Wit and Wisdom

Peterson Perspective: Humor, Wit and Wisdom

Juvenile

Albert: The Cat That Thought He Could Fly

Life Stories (Memoirs)

Legend of Texas Lawman Sammy Long
On the Edge of Night: Finding Love Again at 70 (Vol II Horny Toads Trilogy)
Pansy, The Texas Trapeze Artist
Paths Upon the Prairie
Treating the Texas Town Too Tough to Cry: A True Texas Tale: The Life and Times of
        Doctor James L. Cooper
When Sunsets Glow: Finding Lost Love in Life's Afterglow (Vol III Horny Toads)
Where the Horny Toads Play (Vol I Horny Toads Trilogy)

Politics

American Made Crisis: Aliens in Our Midst
Demolishing the Demons: Theology and Politics Preparing for the New Crusade
Gray Power Politics: Political Wants and Needs of the Newly Powerful Cross-cutting
        Demographic Segment

Relationships

Magnetism to Marriage
Men and Divorce

Major Business Proposals

INF Treaty Portal Monitoring Proposal
Victorville 442-Unit Apartment Complex

Special Accolades

Featured Writer, Western Writers, 2014.
Featured Writer, Society of Classical Poets. Journal, 2019.
Featured Writer, Society of Classical Poets. Journal, 2020.

Unclassified Military Intelligence Officer, Russian Foreign Area Officer, Diplomatic and Business Accomplishments

Note: These are the one I can share though some details may be classified. There are many achievements that will always be classified.

1. **Diego Garcia Base:** In my first assignment with the National Security Agency (NSA), I researched and wrote the majority of a study for the Navy that led them to establish a base on Diego Garcia in the Indian Ocean.

2. **VC Taxation Study:** I wrote the major study of the Viet Cong taxation methods of the South Vietnamese villagers while a Captain and Army advisor in charge of the Phoenix/Phung Hoang program in the Delta of South Vietnam.

3. **Stopped an NVA Division Invasion:** I advised the South Vietnamese Army in 1972 how to blunt an invasion of the Delta Region by a North Vietnamese division of 4,000+ men. Most of them were killed and the invasion failed. I was lauded by my superiors in Saigon.

4. **DIA Methodology:** I wrote the methodology used by the Defense Intelligence Agency (DIA) to analyze all their divisions, personnel numbers, equipment, and types of divisions.

5. **MBFR Analysis and Reporting:** I was the DIA analyst who reported on the strength and divisions of the Group of Soviet Forces, Germany, to the generals negotiating Balanced Force Reductions with the Soviets in Austria.

6. **Spanish Elections:** I wrote a study at the Foreign Area Officer School at Fort Bragg as a student that was provided to the Spanish military from the Pentagon while they were considering whether to intervene in the first democratic election in Spain. My study proved the communists would fall short of the necessary number of

10% of the vote to gain any seat in the new Parliament. The communists failed with less than the 10% required. After that, their popularity decreased to almost nothing.

7. **Grenada:** I uncovered the "New Jewel" communist effort to overtake the Government of the Island Nation of Grenada. Reagan sent troops.

8. **Collection in the Soviet Union:** While an Army Attaché in Moscow, I wrote many classified reports and was told some of them were read by President Reagan. I also collected and reported previously unable to verify intel.

9. **Security Clearances:** I managed all two million (2,000,000) US Army and Civilian military clearances.

10. **Panama:** As the first Military Intelligence and Security Officer attached to the Army Staff, I visited Panama prior to our invasion and provided the plan for how secure our personnel and send out all civilians in advance of any security actions.

11. **Capture of Russian Missile and Codicil Moderator:** As the Portal Monitoring Commander in Votkinsk, Soviet Union, I captured a Russian missile under the terms of the INF Treaty for ten days and prevented it from leaving the area. This caused political and diplomatic repercussions resulting in my moderating a codicil between the US and Soviets of seven changes attached to the original signed treaty.

12. **First Gulf War National Human Intelligence Coordinator:** In the First Gulf War, as a newly retired intelligence officer, I was designated by the Pentagon and intelligence organizations to coordinate all human intelligence collected in Iraq and communicate suggested targets to the Pentagon Air Force bombing planners. I discovered Saddam Hussein rotated to various facilities to spend the night. I coordinated a specific bomb designed to penetrate multi-layered bunkers and targeted him one

night. The bomb did its job and killed 186 Iraqi officials and relatives of Saddam, but he had changed his mind of where to spend that night.

13. **Russian Election Monitor in Russian Far East:** As the First US Foreign Commercial Officer in the Russian East, I was tasked by the US Ambassador to monitor the first Russian elections in Birobidzhan.

14. **Exports:** As the Foreign Commercial Officer in Vladivostok, I brought significant American exports to the region, the size of the continental US by setting up Russian buyer appointments as requested by American exporters.

15. **IBM Regional Sales Manager:** As the First IBM Manager in the Russian Far East, I sold $6,000,000 worth of IBM computers and had another $4,000,000 commitment when I left the next year.

I was on the Full Colonel Promotion List when I retired for a lucrative government contractor offer.

Made in the USA
Columbia, SC
09 September 2024

41345942R00076